Flying Through Houses

Miki Byrne

Indigo Dreams Publishing

First Edition: Flying Through Houses
First published in Great Britain in 2013 by:
Indigo Dreams Publishing
132 Hinckley Road
Stoney Stanton
Leics
LE9 4LN

www.indigodreams.co.uk

ISBN 978-1-909357-06-8

British Library Cataloguing in Publication Data. A CIP record for
this book can be obtained from the British Library.

Designed and typeset in Palatino Linotype by Indigo Dreams.

Cover design by Ronnie Goodyer at Indigo Dreams

Printed and bound in Great Britain by Imprint Academic, Exeter.

Papers used by Indigo Dreams are recyclable products made from
wood grown in sustainable forests following the guidance of the
Forest Stewardship Council.

to Harry

Introduction

Flying Through Houses is an autobiographical collection set in Birmingham, England. The first seventeen poems chart the life of the author by using glimpses of dwellings in which she lived as a child. These memories are more vivid because the author spent only brief times in them. From the age of three months Miki was incarcerated in various hospitals due to serious lung disease. This continued for ten years. After leaving hospital she went to an open-air school for a year. Her parents moved often in an attempt to live in an area that had clean air. The author did not begin formal education until the age of eleven.

Miki spent only six years at home before leaving and giving birth to a daughter. During this time she attended Art School. The homes in which mother and child lived are also described in the poems and it was here that she furthered her education, ultimately gaining two degrees. The sequence of poems ends at the house the author owned until she left to live on a narrow-boat in 1999. Six years later, due to deteriorating health, Miki returned to live on land. She currently lives in Gloucestershire.

Acknowledgements

It has not been easy to compress a long life into thirty-six poems. Too many people to mention have helped to instigate and maintain the process. The few I feel I must mention are: all the poets at Buzzwords, Cheltenham, for their constant support and poetic stimulation, and poets Angela France and Allison Brackenbury for taking the time to read Flying Through Houses and give their comments for the back cover.

The collection would not exist without the support of Dawn Bauling and Ronnie Goodyer, publishers at IDP. I thank them for their faith in me and their support through good times and bad.

The collection itself is dedicated to my husband Harry for his steadfast support as my carer, my husband and literary critic – and also to all the other disabled people who have inspired me not to give up when the going gets tough.

CONTENTS

Flying Through Houses

Where She Lived

She did not live in houses
but flew home to them,
in quick spurts of remembrance
on the wings of wishes
with her parents' blurred faces
laid upon a montage
of overlapping rooms and an address
kept on a scrap of paper
in a wash-bag.
She lived on the end of syringes.
in the ruby drop that trembled
before the needle was discarded.
She lived wrapped around
the silver tips of thermometers
and in other peoples' hands
between the harsh light of morning
and the dimmed lights of the nightshift.
She lived between the last gasp
of a child's breath and cold white
sheets left behind;
between a pillow's crackling starch
and a chilled stethoscope.
Limbo was her place.
Held in that sharp sliver between life
and death, hygiene and bacteria;
all touch clinical as though emotion
would bring contamination
and a smile hold contagion in its open mouth.
She sighed through each day and hoped in vain
to hear the words
'You will be going home soon.'

Blue Baby

Children's Ward, Hill-top Hospital, Bromsgrove,
Worcestershire,1958

On the day of admission, the new girl was silent.
Her violet eyes seemed huge,
shimmering through a lens of unshed tears –
the span of her years numbered
less than a handful.
Her hesitant smile was tinged blue
echoing the pale half-moons of her tiny nails.
A silver fall of fine hair framed her face
and when her eyes closed, the robins-egg curve of lid
was veined like the palest marble.
When they wheeled her bed to Theatre,
the gown swamped her.
She filled less than half of the mattress.
Her face was a winter pansy lying on a drift of snow.
We waved as they pushed her by, her bright hair covered
and notes lying like a slab on the foot of the bed.
The journey was one we had all taken, or would take.
Hours crawled and we passed the time
in our limited ways. Our childish ears were not party
to quiet divulgences, nurses' gossipy speculations.
When shift changed she had not returned.
The windows filled with the blue shadows of dusk
and we asked about her. Nurse Davis could not hold our
gaze or face the expectancy in our hopeful eyes.
She cleared her throat and said
'Do you know where Angels live?'

Clouds Outside

Hill-top Hospital, Bromsgrove, Worcestershire

She feels the mattress firm beneath her back
And she lies in the depths of a white room
Shoulder blades flex, wanting to burst forth
Produce unfolding wings and fly away

Past the bright light, out of the body skywards.
Pillows barely bend under her tender weight
And her chest rises feebly with a rustle like old leaves.
'Raise the bed,' someone says. Postural drainage

Is needed. The back-board clanks, lifts
Is heaved into place in the bright silence.
She is raised from head to waist. Gravity pulls fluids
Adjusts air entry into straining lungs.

She sees clouds outside. She sees sky
Imagines the fresh air she cannot inhale
The soft sun she cannot feel. She lies gasping
And watches as normality passes by.

Walking With Nan
Leighton Rd. Handsworth. Birmingham

Nan was large - firm, like the old teddy, with sawdust in his head and paws worn thin from holding. The girl loved Nan's buttoned-up navy coat that upholstered her, made her feel solid and comfortable, like the old settee in the back room. She loved the dark sparkle of the brooch that lay on the velvet lapel. It was called 'Marcasite.' The word rolled like marmalade on her tongue. She loved walking with her hand grasped in Nanas' plump fingers, pressed by the cushions of flesh that buttressed two gold rings. Granddad had given them. One held a bright diamond.

They would stand at the curb. Always look left, then right. If a car failed to stop quickly enough, or gave the lightest squeak of brakes, Nan would march out, unafraid and stately and crack her walking-cane down on the bonnet. More than a few Morris's and Austin's clanged in Leighton Road, like dropped dustbin lids rolling down the entry. Startled residents would jump. Most drivers would let us cross.

Nan

Leighton Road, Handsworth, Birmingham

Nan lay in the huge wooden bed,
her rotund form a whale in a sea
of candlewick.
It washed in pale green waves
toward her tucked-in feet.
She moved awkwardly,
muscles were slack from lack of use
and her chest wheezed tightly
in the quiet afternoon. Beside her
lay a large black handbag,
the finest, softest leather
from Marshall & Snelgroves. It was
a cornucopia that never left her.

Her Granddaughters' shoes
pattered on the linoleum in the hall
like the rhythmic stumble of summer rain.
She would see Nan for a whole weekend,
allowed home for a brief, joyful respite.
Her small lungs wheezed as badly as Nan's.
The door opened its eye upon the girl.
Young limbs slowly scaled the bed,
snuggled into the talc-scented space where
sheets tented between stomach and mattress.
Little arms hugged her Nan tightly.
Nan opened the bag. The child's face
glowed expectantly, heart a-flutter.
'Are there sweets Nanny?' she whispered.
'I wonder,' she replied, 'I wonder'.

Tenant Street.
Ladywood, Birmingham

She recalls the kitchen: lino green as pond algae, a black block of a stove with curved feet and a deep Belfast sink. Gas mantles on the wall spilt buttery light through small bulbs of net and hissed a sibilant harmony to all their meals. The yard, from her infant height, was huge – paved and walled-in Victorian brick that glistened inkily when it rained. Here she saw her first man in a turban and learned the word 'Sikh'. She wondered if Nana was watching from Heaven to see this delight.

The privy block was outside, shared by every family, wooden seat and squares of newspaper threaded on a string. Her Ma lit a candle at night to repel the cold and reveal the spiders. It was a chilled cavern of shadows but there would be queues in the morning – sleepy-eyed, working men in vests and braces, jutting stubbled chins as they rubbed their goose pimples against the cold.

The wash-house held magic. In its copper a kettle-drum bowl with a lid, as fierce as a gladiator's shield, that shut with a mighty clang. Her brother captured her in it once.
She cried until she was dry, afraid of being cooked while he sat on the lid and laughed. On Mondays women took turns to heat the copper. It bubbled like a cauldron and belched carbolic steam, thick and clinging. She hunkered on the duck-board, breathed in the pungent vapour and wondered how a blue-bag made things white.

On sunny days, the shadows of washing danced like marionettes across the foot-worn brick and daisies grasped a tiny hold on life in the cracks. It was a fortress, backed all around by houses, with the neighbours known and always spoken to with respect. The only way in was through their back doors or down the dark, arched entry that echoed a long run of steps out to Tenant Street.

New Shoes, 1958

May gently smoothed the cheap paper against the table,
pressed the fold-lines flat with the pads of her fingers
and breathed the antiseptic smell that ghosted
from the brown envelope.
She gazed at the outline of the small foot,
drawn in smudged pencil.
The line was broken in a few places.
It was more poignant than any photograph.

Her daughter's name scrawled jaggedly across one corner
in a hand too adult and ferocious to be her child's. The
sketch came unaccompanied by letter or salutation.
She could imagine her little girl fidgeting as her foot was
firmly held and the wriggling of her white-socked toes.
May had bought the new shoes.
Brown and sensible with a good thick sole.

She had judged the size. Carefully placed
a shoe over the drawing then increased up to allow for growth.
The parcel had been posted the day before and May had
haughtily ignored the postmistress's curiosity.
Now she placed the sketch in the kitchen drawer.
It would lie there with the others,
until a new one arrived next year.

Off the Train

The train pulls out.
A whisper of noise hovers.
The platform is an open plain.
Wreathed in wraiths of steam.
The girl is small and he
stands beside her. Tall.
Familiar and yet unknown.
Her hand in his is cold.
She shivers and waits.
Eyes large, heart pounding.
He steps forward.
The tug of his hand
Unbreakable.
She follows, blue-cloaked
by his cigarette smoke.
And he tells her he is
her Father.

Where is Auntie Rose?
Aunt Anne's House, Oxford St., Stirchley, Birmingham

Ma all but dragged her to Auntie Anne's house. All frown and hustle, fussing her into a coat. The other Aunts arrived as if by magic, breathless and without their hats. There was a feeling in the air, whispers over her head. Aunt Maureen hissed about 'little pitchers' and 'big ears' and Auntie Rose had done something stupid. The girl puzzled over hushed tones and women gathered like crows shuffling round a corpse, their hands aflutter at throats and mouths.

They left her to play with a jewellery box. She sat on an acre of candlewick, grasped odd sentences from the half-closed door. Muffled weeping seeped in to make her fearful. She trickled fine chains through her fingers and breathed a faint tang of '4711'. Her Ma took charge as always and the girl asked what Auntie Rose had done and *why* was it a sin?

The world fell silent. The Aunts sharp glances duelled over her head. Pale handkerchiefs were lifted. She was in a cross fire of moist looks. Aunt Phyllis tempted her with biscuits and led her to the kitchen by a cold hand. Over the years she puzzled about Aunt Rose's sinful act. She promised herself that when she was older she would ask her. Curiosity itched but she never found Auntie Rose again.

First Sight

Reginald Rd. Saltley Birmingham

She watched them walk up the hill
Visible from the turn off to the High street.
Cars were scarce then. Her view was clear.
These were the invaders. Cousins

Coming from Ireland to lodge with them,
Fill their rooms, break their toys.
Auntie Peg and Uncle Kevin walked behind
their children up the slope of Reginald Road

Like two collies herding sheep –
Hilary on the left: short, with a straight fringe,
Declan on the right: mop-headed and small.
In the middle walked Joyce: a teenager

Tall and poised, white socked and gloved,
Good coat and communion dress underneath.
Auntie Peg's hand lay on her shoulder.
The girl just knew that Joyce would boss her about.

And carried carefully in Joyce's hand,
Arm angled against the weight,
A golden canary in a cage
Trilled its song into the dull afternoon.

Girl on a Bomb-peck

She feels that this world is from a grim tale
where giants have pulled the buildings apart
in a fury of spite. There is desolation in the air,
in precious things left torn and strewn.
She gazes in wonder at random destruction,
at half a sink that hangs by a bolt on a wall
and a big bed skewed – to jut in precarious balance
over a high and listing floor.
A tattered sheet flaps in grubby desolation.
She climbs hesitantly over piles of bricks.
A two-story chimney breast stands on its own
casting a deep shadow that she does not cross.
A rag of curtain droops through an empty window.
She wonders who slept in the room
where pigeons roost and dust sifts down.
The gardens are scattered, hurled
by explosives into a spray of dust and seeds.
Yet some have made a haphazard return.
Lupins grow in a doorway flanked by a black stove
upside down, its door ajar for rats to scurry in.
She edges past, afraid of the dark aperture.
A jagged stairway points into the empty sky.
She picks through debris to find anything whole,
any intact item to show that someone had lived here.
All around her are shards and shattered things.
Sadness encroaches. It seeps in like the like dirty water
leaching into her shoes and socks.
The Rose-bay willow-herb pushes through a holed bucket
and the smell of catmint rises beneath her feet.

Ingoldsby Road
Northfield, Birmingham

A thump down the stairs to the front door –
the risers tall to her and the handrail a reach away.
'It's a Maisonette,' her Ma had said with pride
but it was just a flat: square, utility, up one flight.

At the end of the street slouched a line of 1960's boxes:
poured, reinforced, cast, butted against each other,
rust beginning to ooze through as if they were bleeding.
Gaps in between led to washing lines and bicycles.

The Council concreted over the grass verge as a sop
to progress and the line of plate glassed shops
indulged more pouring, in the upright pillars and cast
flower tubs filled with stones and not a bloom in sight.

She climbed on one once and twisted her ankle jumping off.
The Newsagents window was scabbed with postcards
advertising second hand spin driers, baby clothes, a job
delivering leaflets. At the bottom of the hill the playing field

was their arena, surrounded by a water-filled ditch,
midge-covered in summer. Frozen in winter
white air bubbles pressed to its surface.
Her little sister fell through it one year.
She carried her cold and crying all the way home.

Waiting for a Train.
Ingoldsby Rd., Northfield, Birmingham

This new home had a garden,
a tangle of weeds that stretched long and narrow
sharply square-ended by the railway line.
At first, the wheel-thunder frightened her.
It jerked her from warm dreams,
where she was a Princess and owned
the smiling doll that Ma would buy her-one day.
Later, she found a hole in the fence.
If she bent her knees slightly, she could put her eye to it.
She grew to remember the times,
to recognise the slight signals,
the minute change in the air
and she would run
to place her face against rough wood,
breath in the tang of old creosote.
She loved the gut-tingling
waiting.
the faraway *chickety-chack, chickety-chack*
that built to a trembling underfoot,
a slight quiver in the fence then a huge, racketing *whoosh*
and the breath-snatching, rattling roar,
a blur of windows, faces, wheels.
Gone in seconds
with the silence hurling back so quickly it might all
never have happened.

Her eye at the knot hole would water.
As if someone had blown salt through it.

Accidentally Safe

Ingoldsby Rd., Northfield, Birmingham

She struggles to keep up,
breath rasps in her chest,
back hunches from the strain.
Her scars pull every time
she turns the handlebars
and her legs ache.
A car approaches, impatient,
a little too fast,
nears the spilling shadow
of the railway bridge.
It swerves, grazes her back wheel
and she falls,
disappears beneath the bumper
as if the car has somehow eaten her up.
The friends stop, turn.
Someone screams.
The driver climbs out, eyes huge,
denials spilling from his bloodless lips.
Someone peers underneath.
There she lies. A small curl of limbs,
smack in the centre of all four wheels.
The bike was written off.

Broken – The Girl in the Care Home Garden

Cropwood Open-air School, Blackwell, Worcestershire

The song could be heard across the garden
wafting through speckled Laurels
drifting over cerise Rhododendrons
always the same – over and over.

Shine on Harvest Moon – incongruous words.
carried on a voice drenched in melancholy.
The child sang every day but only in solitude.
hidden by foliage, enclosed by shrubbery.

The girl found her once. The songstress would not speak.
Her eyes were splintered crystals – unfocussed, bleak.
her understanding fragmented. She moved on
into oblivion. Her mind scarred and broken.

White Sinks.

Cropwood Open-air School, Blackwell, Worcestershire

A row of white sinks stand straight as piano keys.
Copper pipes arc above clad in scabs of verdigris.
Facing them, a line of young girls step forward,
conscious of their nakedness.
Holding name-tagged flannels, they dip and squeeze,
rub under arms, swipe across napes, dab between legs.
Some sense the glances cast by Miss as her eyes
caress their smooth buttocks, their tiny bird-wing
shoulder-blades. In line, they step back, goose-pimpled,
choreographed by embarrassment. They stand and shiver,
small hands held modestly over smooth pubic mounds.
They wait for instructions like automatons, Pavlovian
in their response. Rough towels are distributed.
Skin quickly rubbed back to warmth.
The order to move is snapped –
a bark, full of indecipherable nuances.
Girls grab white cotton underwear
and dress in silence.

Dormitory
Cropwood Open-air School, Blackwell, Worcestershire

She waits in the dark, jumps at noises,
at the winds whistle and the curtains wing-like flap.
Loneliness spears her though others sleep close by.
Chilled air falls heavy as a penance
whilst she waits many hours for sleep
screwing her eyes tight and pulling the one
thin blanket under her chin. It gives no comfort
and the pale rosary lies limp in her grip.
Her freezing toes protrude, bone-pale in the dark.
Fear blossoms. It combines with the cold
to roughen her skin to the texture of grit.
A frigid breeze blows through windows that are closed
only on pain of punishment. Steps on the landing echo.
They pause by the door. Listening. In this place
all doors remain unlocked, privacy is forbidden.
The door opens. A long shadow slithers in.
The girl cringes. Her bed is her prison,
the bars defined by terrified expectancy.
Her head burrows into a thin pillow
wet with salt and hopelessness.
She knuckles her fist to her mouth as muffled sobs
spiral around dark walls
to disappear into inevitability.

Living in Hope
Cropwood Open-air School, Blackwell, Worcestershire

She doesn't recall the exact staggering moment
when time warped and she became Oliver Twist –
not clothed in rags, not exactly starving
though the Artful Dodger could be seen
in a few of her companions.
Yet she was worked, disciplined, placed in
a cold dormitory with strangers as if in a novel.
She was told that this place was good for her,
though dew-damp walls and staff
with bruising hands put the lie to that.
She would imagine that she was someone else,
built a small leafy house under the hedge
and talked to a squirrel,
took food from the tea table to keep him coming,
pretending that she was a character in a well-read tale
and that the hero would one day arrive shining,
brave and in the nick of time.
As life follows its own course she was not surprised
when no-one came. Yet hope would blossom,
grow tall in the soil of her optimism,
be felled by the axe
of disappointment and grow again. After all,
Oliver found his escape.

Clutter and Dust
113, Lockwood Road, Northfield, Birmingham

This was her first real home. One that lasted more than a weekend. They had moved from next door. Ma and Da hefted their furniture over the palings from one back garden to another. The move was something she puzzled over and was told it was for garage space. Another oddity to accept when she returned from Open Air-School for the last time with cropped hair and no sense of belonging.

This house meant Secondary School and skirts rolled over at the top, Mary Quant and wanting to be grown up, punctuated by weeks of lying on the day-bed, choked by bronchitis or pneumonia each winter while the television blared through her delirium. One term she returned to school to find her class had collected for a wreath.
They had heard she was dead.

After work her Ma would take her stockings off and stuff them rolled up, behind a cushion with her girdle and a bottle of sherry. There was clutter and dust – too many things in a small space and the poltergeist that thumped the door from inside the disused pantry. Her Da reeked of smoke and sat by the fire surrounded by a ring of beer bottles they were not allowed to touch.

He carried horrors in his mind from the war that he would never relate but consistently tried to drown. From here she took her sister to school and back, took herself to the roller rink and the chip-shop, wore pop-art dresses and climbed back into the house through the bathroom window when she was late. This place was time spent alone while her Ma worked all hours at the psychiatric hospital.

Ma smelt of Largactyl and rotated her uniforms for hygiene's sake. Washing them was a ritual and the prized Sister's cuffs and cap were always spotless. There was housework, minding her little sister and ironing shirts for her brother – he would give her Chinese burns if she didn't. It was Christmases and red baubles, the allotments at the garden's end, first job, first walkout and Art School. It was all her plans shattered in the explosion of her parent's fury when she became pregnant and they threw her out.

Milk and Blarney
Lockwood Rd., Northfield, Birmingham

The little people lived at the
end of the garden.
Her Da often told her tales of them.
The two of them left a drop of milk out

on Sundays and birthdays.
Placed behind the shed,
or tucked down by the fence.
She would look for the Leprechauns

day after day. Not a hard task
in a council house patch.
Yet, they must have hidden.
She would sit still as a stone

watching with hopeful eyes
as pigeons flapped above her
and the sounds of the allotment
drifted through the hedge.

She would hear the clunk of a spade.
The murmur of male voices
wrapped in pipe smoke.
It curled through the privet

and smelled of burnt plums.
She waited, often until sundown
'till the gardeners had gone
and Ma called her in for dinner.

She saw nothing of the little ones.
Not a flicker. But sometimes,
just now and then, as she stood
and brushed her skirt clean

and her knee-bones clicked from sitting
too long, she would be still
and hear, like a tickle in her ear,
the faintest, tinkling laugh.

A Small Act of Defiance
Da, Lockwood Rd., Northfield, Birmingham

The overalls were blue, washed to faded shadows
like pieces of captured sky. They fell into folds worn into
their own memory. The boots were hard, toe-tecting bulbous
humps that crouched upon his feet-like pigs noses with mud
and diesel layered thick upon them, souvenirs of demolition
sites, stomped over through unrelenting days of graft. His
shirt was sometimes frayed, laundered to a threadbare
softness. His hands showed his trade in the contour lines of
grease that circled his knuckles and defied soap and bristle.
Yellow stains of nicotine wrapped fingers used to crooking
around a snooker cue and the smell of Brylcreme would waft
from his thick hair always kept military neat. He would
sometimes feel dark and twisted plagued by flashbacks and
thoughts of the bayonet kept under the pillow. He would
often be hung-over, dying for a lunch-time pint to resurrect
the euphoria of last night's skin-full. Some days he would be
bored with mooching round the yard, waiting at the
foreman's will for work to be allocated, knowing but never
saying, that the Irish were given last and that 'Paddy' was a
label he loathed. He and 'da boys' would trade tall tales and
Woodbines. Yet, the dickie-bow was always in place –
rakish, incongruous, the colour of red roses. It sat beneath
his stubbled chin and shone like a beacon across the dull
wasteland of the site. It was his proud 'up yours' to the
world and to all the gobshites he hated within it.

\

Top of the Milk

Lockwood Rd., Northfield, Birmingham

One pint Saturdays – gold top
placed on the doorstep, brought in quick
before the urchin birds could peck the foil

and steal the cream,
taking tiny sips through their sharp
little beaks while their flirting tails

made see-saw bobs. We would vie
for that cream: me for cornflakes,
the cat for its own sake whilst she

rubbed figures of eight around our
legs in hope. My brother wanted it for
coffee but it was Ma's – her treat,

taken as it came, each velvet swallow
savoured, 'till all that remained was just milk
and a white line across her upper lip.

Round the Block at Night
Auntie Peg's house, Oxford St., Digbeth, Birmingham

They ran – down to the Old Wharf Tavern. Her Da was drinking. She heard his mouth-organ wheeze. Mingled with the laugh and lilt of Irish voices. His feet would be itching to dance. Quivering, they slowed to inch past, backs to the wall, palms against cold brick. All with the same thought *She'll catch us! We'll all get thraiped!* Delicious fear blossomed inside them. Then,

a scuttle under the railway arches, high buttressed caverns of black brick that shouldered the bed factory where Aunt Peg cleaned in the evenings. The stench of the knacker's yard two streets over, made them gag and brought a taste of death on the night air. They skittered on, through a mist of clinging drizzle, pinching their wet noses and jostling each other as if they did this all the time.

They were a commando night-raid and made guns with two fingers pointing. They hurtled pell-mell into the night, dared the sucking dark of alleys and the danger of evening streets, past windows where silhouettes rose and dark houses hunkered down. They crept along the inky tunnel of the entry, back towards their yard. The cobbles were slick and the wash-house door hung open, like a great murky maw ready to swallow them. They braved its devouring jaws and slithered by

eyes fixed on the black hollow inside to keep watch for the grizzly night-monster that crouched within and craved their pumping hearts. Chickens clucked behind sagging wire; evil demons screeching them home. Time had stretched. It felt so late. Yet the kitchen was lit and someone was up – Auntie Peg with her tea and a fag. Their faces set in contrition, they crept back, to take what she might dish out.

Something Triggered a Memory
Auntie Peg's House, Oxford St., Digbeth, Birmingham

As the storm breathed its last, the tingle of ozone twitched a memory awake. It brought pictures of Auntie Peg's cellar – our den. Warmed by the belly of a glowing paraffin stove, the sly shimmer of heat heightened the dark aromas that rose up. Burning fuel clogged our noses, fought with the earthy smell of damp that oozed from the floor. Specks of coal dust fell upon the stove and sparked in a tiny flickering display. The walls were crumbly. Lazily shed chalky flakes of white-wash and the greenish tang of lime prickled our throats.

Coal dust invaded our mouths and noses, settled as a dark outline around bricks. The taste of it crackled saltily upon our tongues. Corners were impenetrable and poked at our fear of the dark, causing shivers to tip-toe across our napes. Light fell like an avalanche, through a street-level grating. The coal clattered and rattled through into a stygian, shadow-sucking heap. The stove sighed out little heat and a feeble Halloween glow. The bitterness of hot metal hung on the air as we huddled like refugees and listened to the sounds of feet above.

Watched shadows slide down the walls, to slither away in the length of a stride. Occasional words drifted down to us, like feathers from quarrelsome birds. We held our breath, rigid with the thrill of eavesdropping. Stifled giggles – wondering if the voices were aware of us, as we swapped gruesome tales to scare each other, with chunks of bread and dripping, greasy in our fists. Smudge-faced urchins, we held hands in childish conspiracy. And upstairs, Auntie Peg made tea and counted a few pennies into her purse.

The Knackers Yard
Auntie Peg's House, Oxford St., Digbeth., Birmingham

He wanted to show her the knackers yard.
His big-cousin bravado steered them
under the rattling gloom of the railway arch,
past the smoky half-glass walls of the bottling plant
and the mountain of metal grotesques
that loomed over the scrappers' corrugated fence.
As they approached, the stench hit her like a club,
then became a wet and rotting rag over her face.
She gagged as she gazed at the rivulets
of blood water that flowed from under the knackers gate.
He dared her to step in it. Her stomach flipped
and she pushed him away as he laughed.
They put their eyes to the gap. Her heart thudded.
Piles of stained skins grew like bizarre fungi,
leaking blood and salt. More salt sat
in dirty crystalline hillocks. Gore splattered men
in aprons and high boots joked and flung fleeces
and leather about. Her eyes filled.
These had been animals, living farmyard creatures
now rendered to stinking parodies of their former shape.
Her face crumpled. He said
'Ah, Jesus! What the feck are ye cryin' for?'

Ley Hill Park
Ley Hill, Northfield, Birmingham

We gazed down the hill,
poised upon the windswept crest.
Me on my Moulton, June ready to run
grinning like a demon with her pale hair wild.
Before us the long slick slope rolled away,
abruptly curtailed at the bottom of its green curve
by a horizontal path beside a stream.
We had felt that swift water
untangled each others' blood-striped limbs
from ropes of brambles,
always brought hankies to pat up the blood.
The trick wasn't in the ride, or the run
but in the stopping,
the wrenching of handlebars sharp left or right
eyes closed against the vicious spray of stones.
We had scabby knees and fading bruise-shadows.
We took a deep breath for a mighty, lung-stretching yell
and flew.

Moulton is a brand of bicycle that had small wheels.

Rheumatology Waiting Room
Selly Oak Hospital, Birmingham

Hard chairs stand pushed against pale walls
to make a corral for the desperate,
fenced by closed windows and stands of leaflets
that bend listlessly in a parody of the patients who wait.
We sit slumped in dejected attitudes. Pain etched
into our faces, by the acid press of suffering.
Necks bend in the grip of ankylosing spondylitis,
backs show scoliosis curves,
hands gnarl in the slow process of subluxation.
Disease twists us, pushes our bodies
beyond normal parameters. In a paradox of nature
our own immune systems attempt to destroy us.
Fear lurks behind many expressions – boredom, resignation
sketched by turned-down eyes and mouths.
We are familiar with this, have integrated it into life
resigned to no cure and carrying the weight of disability.
Whole life stories stand written in lines of experience,
in the grazing rub of attrition – skills eroded and jobs lost.
The waiting is inevitable – each minute a step
toward treatment that has no guarantee but comes
wrapped in optimism. We wait
propped up by stoic patience. Hope always
shines here but is not always fulfilled.

Ray's Bedsit
Park Hill, Moseley, Birmingham

The room was two flights up,
stairs dingy and dangerously unlit.

It was a box let to the desperate by
the unscrupulous. Indistinct wallpaper

once a patterned blue but faded
to the colour of a healing bruise.

A single bed stood against the wall,
with cheap blankets and

a second-hand lamp beside it.
Shirts hung on wire hangers

suspended from the dado rail
like disembodied torsos.

Beatles songs flowed from an old Dansette
and musty air butted against a window

painted shut. A single gas ring glowed
eerily blue as they lay in the dark and

one-pan meals became staple.
In this room he first touched her,

whispered promises and made her believe.
She ignored the drabness,

clothed it in romance and never dreamed
that one day she would come to hate him.

Second Bedsit
Park Hill, Moseley, Birmingham

This was the place she ran to
fuelled by desperation and with an embryo
fluttering inside her. The rain fell
straight as blades and glistened in the lights
of the garage, their room perched above
like a ragged nest in a battered city tree.
On the ground, rainbows rippled from spilt fuel.
Her Da pulled up to vent his Catholic wrath.
He flung open the back doors of the car,
leaned in and pushed all her belongings
out into the night. Clothes flopped
like broken-winged birds in the wind.
Small items tinkled and rolled, making circles
in the deepening wash of the downpour.
His shouted monologue flung words
like stones toward the window where she peered.
'Whore! Hussy! Slut!' punctuated the night
and her heart.
Other drivers turned away
in embarrassment. She burned with shame
and later, crept down to rescue meagre things
from neon puddles.

Giving Birth in 1969

Sorrento Maternity Hospital, Wake Green Rd., Moseley, Birmingham

When her child was dragged mewling from her body
without the help of medication and with no company
but the judgement of others, she was resentful; exhausted,
wanted to forget the days of pain and sink into dark oblivion.

She lay in that birthing bed afraid, too young, knowing
nothing but her own conviction. She was the object of
nurses' quiet scorn and her parents' embarrassed fury.
She listened to the thunder and the rain that echoed her
tempestuous despair.

The stigma of being alone marked her like a never-ending
bruise. Post-natal depression smothered her. She was
drenched in fear – of life, of her errant husband, of poverty,
of human nature itself. The infant would not feed and her
cries were like nails on a blackboard.

She and the baby struggled through that first winter, alone
for days, cold to the bone and with misery making a cage
that could not be unlocked. For a long time death was
appealing and guilt dragged her like an anchor. Her attempt
to end her life failed

gained her only her husband's anger and a slap for comfort.
Her pain, her shame, consolidated by society and parental
disdain into a weight too heavy to hold. She had embraced
free-love and found that all love had its price. She paid it
every day.

First Flat
Beaconsfield Rd., Balsall Heath, Birmingham

Random rooms
on the ground floor of a house –
a choppy conversion
that left one room uninhabitable:
the dripping no-man's-land
between bedroom and kitchen.
She painted walls cerise,
made curtains with Rag Market bargains,
placed a speckled mirror over the mantelpiece
to enlarge the room.
She nursed her child here,
worried that the damp might kill her,
Carrying her to the clinic at Mary Street
in all weathers.
She found a dead chicken on the doorstep once.
Another time a burglar in the kitchen,
who ran when she raged at him.
She sat by the locked door with the baby in her arms.
'till the sun came up
and she could walk to the phone-box
without being accosted as a prostitute.

Flat at Chelmsley Wood

Her Ma thought they were lucky
when they were offered the flat:
a brand new-build but sterile
out in the wasteland of a new estate,
isolated and barren
with only an hourly Midland Red
to link them to familiarity.
They filled this pristine place with tat.
They owned nothing else.
There was under-floor heating
that they could not afford and large windows
that looked out onto washing lines,
bleak paved areas where kids smoked
and dogs peed.
This was hours away from all she knew,
friendless and soulless,
a prison for her and her child
and paradise for her husband who beat her
whenever the mood took him
and used the isolation as a set of chains
to bind her with.
Sparse as it was, pride drove her
to clean it till it shone,
in the hours before she wrapped up her child
and they left him.

Tamerton Road Flat
Bartley Green, Birmingham

Another concrete box – grey and grimed.
How councils loved concrete then
and happily poured them into it,
four floors up with balconies.
Always extreme. An oven in summer

but in winter the condensation would
stream from the window sills.
Carpets soaked and stank for days
and on the inside, ice would form
making fairy patterns that grew by the day.

The rooms dwarfed their belongings.
Mother and child gradually grew into them
adding finds from charity shops
and filling every space with plants.
The gas fire hissed and the hall was

a cold corridor: windowless, dark.
The view though, was a gift.
They looked across Senely's Park
as if standing on the bridge of a great ship.
Stretches of grass were cresting green waves
that glistened and rippled before them.

They could see all the way to Bangham Pit
to the shimmering silver of the reservoir.
Across to the left were other blocks.
Just close enough to see the Police arrive one day
to take a man with a shotgun away

88, Gleave Rd
Selly Oak, Birmingham

This house held the best and worst.
A little Victorian terrace, with hers snugged in
at the end, a matchbox garden and a money-pit
from the day of signing. She held lovers here,
knowing peace in intermittent pools of comfort.

The builders that fixed the roof were rogue
and she stood in a dark thunderstorm one night.
holding tight to a sail of tarpaulin that lifted her
off her feet in the muddy loft-space.
She held parties in this house,

packed rooms on birthdays and New Years –
finger food and cans. Her daughter's room
filled with teenagers drinking stolen lager
they thought had gone unseen.
She married again from here. The secret let out

and a celebration made. It was unwanted but
accepted gladly as it was kindly given.
The marriage crumbled there, with him away
so much in the band and all his affairs coming back
to haunt them. She grew weaker and stronger,

lost a career and gained a disability,
learned to drive and had to give it up,
took on challenges and left her beauty
impressed upon the houses walls.
She made the garden a little piece of heaven,
digging up one hundred old bricks alone.

She made friends and became used to the weird way
that voices would bounce round the cul-de-sac
although in the eighteen years she lived here
she never found out why the locals called it
'The Pudding Bag.'

Bears and Dippers

Her days are measured by the sky
as it rises and falls
in its glow from streaking sunrise
to the softest slide of evening.
Her friends are the clouds
that wave their sleeves as they pass
and the rain that drips tear-shapes
to slither down the window-pane.
Sometimes the wind will call.
It pulls and entices, strokes her face,
slides perfume through her window
on summer nights.
It asks her to walk in the dew-silvered grass
and in winter, when the snow falls,
she watches its crystalline dance.
The sky-colours come and go and starry nights
are her favourite.
She looks for bears and dippers in the black dome
and hopes that Orion is smiling.
She knows the names of clouds and can smell
when sleet is coming.
She sees through a square-paned eye,
in a few degrees of turning.
Her vision is tuned to the vagaries of light
And she can tell the time by a depth of darkness
or a shadow's slant
through the curtain's thoughtless gape.

Changing Lives
88, Gleave Rd., Selly Oak, Birmingham – Narrowboat *Amadeus*

To leave was unheard of. To split and disperse possessions
that bulged with memories and the love of others' hearts.
It pained her to reject the pride given by this home;
the warming glow of achievement.
It had stiffened her spine and formed her into the shape she
now was. The anchor of belonging held her fast but to him,
it was just a house. She struggled,
like a fly in the web of another's dream,
felt tied by ropes of friendship and familiarity.
A piece of her heart was buried in the tiny garden
she had bent her back in, along with the grave of a tabby cat
who held love in every movement.
A compromise was reached, tenants found, set in place so
that this refuge could sit as comfort at the back of her mind.
The sharp edge of adventure was accepted, all ties cut
as they trembled on the edge of a new life.
His enthusiasm washed over her like a wave.
She began to believe, to think that taking him back had been
the right choice. Ahead, the waterways beckoned –
a wild and beautiful dream.
She pictured the graceful droop of a willow, the scything dip
of swallows, a life of travel, anonymity,
to drop out like a child of the sixties should –
no address, no council tax and the peace of flowing water.
They became boat-dwellers alight with the fire of discovery.
Yet, as they progressed it was he who became disillusioned.
After he left she found peace,
laughed at her old fears., travelling on like an Undine
alone and singing as one
with the water.

Indigo Dreams Publishing
132, Hinckley Road
Stoney Stanton
Leicestershire
LE9 4LN
www.indigodreams.co.uk